RIO GRANDE

BY ROBERT REYNOLDS

TEXT BY TONY HILLERMAN

International Standard Book Number 0-912856-18-1
Library of Congress Catalog Card Number 74-33863
Copyright© 1975 by Publisher • Charles H. Belding
Graphic Arts Center Publishing Co.
2000 N.W. Wilson • Portland, Oregon 97209 • 503/224-7777
Designer • Robert Reynolds
Printer • Graphic Arts Center
Bindery • Lincoln & Allen
Printed in the United States of America

White Rock Canyon, New Mexico

Arroyo Hondo, New Mexico

Aspen leaves, upper Rio Grande, Colorado

Lower Rio Grande valley, McAllen, Texas

Mesa west of Albuquerque, New Mexico

Santa Elena Canyon, Big Bend National Park, Texas □ Clouds over Sierra Nacimiento, New Mexico

061590

Howard County Library
Big Spring, Texas

Church in Acoma Pueblo, New Mexico

Crusted snow, San Luis Valley, Colorado

Aspen leaf in summer snow, Colorado

RIO GRANDE

It begins at the Continental Divide, on the backbone of North America, and its 1,900-mile journey to the Gulf of Mexico makes it second only to the Missouri-Mississippi in length among the continent's rivers. It drains a quarter-million square miles of the Southern Rockies, the Southwest and Mexico. Yet in certain places and in certain seasons one can walk across its bed and get nothing on his shoes but dust. Of all the world's great rivers only the water of the Ganges is more heavily used to irrigate crops. Yet in 1970 Congress made it the first stream officially named a ''wild river'' to preserve its still untouched canyons for those who love the wilderness. At places it is a clear, cold trout stream. At others it is grey with silt, or orange with the mud from the Rio Chama, drained dry by irrigation diversion, or green with explosive growth of algae and other water plants. We call it the Rio Grande but on Mexican maps it is the Rio Bravo. It has had at least a dozen other names. Alonso Alvarez de Piñeda sailed his galleon into its mouth in 1519 and called it Rio de las Palmas in recognition of the jungle of palm trees that covered its delta. The scouts of Don Juan de Oñate found it a thousand miles upstream in 1598 when the May floods were roaring down from the mountains. After it drowned two of their horses, they named it Rio Bravo del Norte—the Wild River of the North. A sailor shipwrecked from the fleet of Francis Drake crossed it in what is now South Texas and, charmed by its serene lushness, called it the River of May. I have lived along it much of my life, studied it, fished it, washed in it, floated down it, and it seems to me that no American river can match the richness of its history, its variety, or its power to stir the imagination.

The source of the Rio Grande is a high horseshoe valley just under Stony and Humpback passes in the San Juan Mountains of southern Colorado. I was last here on September 21—the last day of summer and the beginning of fall. But at almost two and a half miles above sea level the few days that pass for summer are far behind and there's not much left of autumn. Behind me Pole Mountain rises to 13,740 feet. To the northeast Bent, Cuba and Carson Peaks, all well over 13,000, form the horizon. The south is walled off by the Rio Grande Pyramids, which reach to almost 14,000 feet. To the west stand Canby, Hunchback and Nebo Peaks, connected by saddleback passes. Inside this sky-high enclosure is an irregular grassy depression, more than ten miles across. Its upper margins are the broken grey of talus slopes, spotted and streaked with the white of snowbacks, which summer is never quite long enough to melt. (If you dig deep enough through the hard late-summer snow you encounter blue-white ice left over, perhaps, from the Age of Glaciers.) But most of the immense bowl is the muted green of the life zone biologists call Arctic-Alpine. Here grow the quick seeding sedges, the short, tough tundra grasses, and, along the streams, squat durable bushes and the reeds and tuberous plants that flourish in the dank soil where cold water seeps. Here no plant grows that cannot survive high winds, 60-below zero F temperatures and the crushing burden of compacted snow.

The world here is too harsh for most mammals. Even the snowshoe rabbit and the ubiquitous chipmunk tend to stick to protection of timberline far below. The sheep driven up the old Rocky Pass trail after the spring thaws are driven out again before the first heavy snows. One sees few birds. Now and then a golden eagle will drift overhead, but he's headed for better hunting down the slopes. An occasional Clark's nutcracker, pine grosbeak or rosy finch has staked out temporary feeding territory among the brushy places. But the only live thing which seems comfortably at home here is the pika. They move among the boulders like animated balls of brown fur, their whistling calls loud in the silence.

But even when the breeze (and the pikas) are still, the silence here is not quite absolute. There is always the sound of water. The water is everywhere. It dribbles down from hundreds of springs and seeps to feed scores of little brooks, which combine to become Bear Creek, Pole Creek, and Middle Pole, and West Pole, and Quartzite, and the myriad arms of Deep Creek and, finally, where Deep and Pole merge under Timber Hill, the Rio Grande itself. Even when the heavy snows of autumn bury these streams, the muted sound of water-over-stone can still be heard. The modern record for snowfall on the Rio Grande watershed was set in the winter of 1951-1952, when an estimated 55 feet (enough to bury a five-story building) fell on Wolf Creek Pass. When measured on April 1, the snowpack, despite evaporation loss, melt, and the winter-long compression under its own crushing weight, was still 131 inches deep. It contained 55.3 inches of water and the average Rocky Mountain snowfall contains one inch of water for one foot of snowfall.

It's difficult on a sunny autumn day to imagine Stony Pass basin buried under such an immensity of snow. It's even harder to visualize how different this valley will be when spring arrives and the high country begins to release this wealth of water. Every slope and hillside will be shiny then with the wetness of melting snow. The brooks that now barely trickle will be gushing. The network of creeks will flood with murky runoff. The faint music made by the exhausted streams of autumn will be replaced by the roar of cataracts.

The runoff season extends from early spring in the foothills to midsummer in the highest of the high country—but the heavy snowmelt period is usually compressed into a period of about 40 days. In that span, after an average year of snowfall, an incredible 500 million tons of water comes thundering down the mountain tributaries into the mainstream of the Great River. After a wet winter, runoff sometimes exceeds a billion tons.

Before this runoff was checked, the Rio Grande in spring deserved the title "Rio Bravo." Its floods were wild indeed, making investment in irrigation works a risky business and the life expectancy of bridges short. A group of San Luis Valley farmers joined forces shortly before World War I to apply the first curb. Using mule power and packed-in supplies, they built the tower pile of earth that blocks the narrow slot between Finger Mesa and Simpson Mountain. On this quiet

autumn day, the reservoir behind Farmer's Union Dam has been drained almost empty. The river snakes for miles through a bottom flattened by 60 years of silting and greened now by a quick growth of algae. From the dirt road that hugs the slope above it, the Rio Grande here looks like a silver snake on a billiard table. But by early next summer, this narrow valley will be filled with 50,000 acre feet of water in a lake eight miles long.

When it leaves this dam, the Rio Grande has traveled only a dozen miles from its origins. But it has already dropped more than 3,000 feet to the 9,350 foot level—squandering 20 per cent of the altitude it will use to carry it halfway across America. The Rio Grande here is every man's dream of what a mountain river should be. And thus it remains for 50 miles. It runs over a clean bottom of gravel and polished boulders. It is cold, clear, rich in oxygen and alive with rainbow trout—a stream of rapids and deep pools and driftwood on its banks for fires to warm the fly-fishermen. It is hemmed in by mountains, with the La Garita Wild Area to the north and the San Juan Primitive Area to the south. The treeless tundra of the Arctic-Alpine Zone is now far behind. The river has dropped quickly through the Hudsonian life zone—at this latitude a narrow belt of "wind timber" (stunted fir, Englemann spruce, white-barked pine and mountain hemlock). It has dropped past Shotgun Mountain into the great Upland Meadow, where for the first time its water is diverted to irrigate an expanse of hay fields. It circles the lonely eminence of Bristol Head Mountain and runs—for the only time in its long journey—almost due north toward Creede—the last of the boom silver towns, which crowds the narrow canyon of Willow Creek.

Creede is the capital and metropolis of the upper river—a village for which the map claims 350 residents. Its little schoolhouse serves a few score children scattered through an area not much smaller than Connecticut. In the summer it is busy with fishermen and tourists. Now it is quiet, bracing for winter. Woodpiles tower beside houses, and in the Snowshoe Cafe the talk is of the brown bear that has been raiding garbage cans—fattening himself for hibernation.

Eight miles below Creede, the river pours through Wagon Wheel Gap. Reinforced by the waters of Goose Creek, South Fork, and Embargo Creek, it flows out into one of America's great intermountain parks—the San Luis Valley. Here the landscape, and the river, change drastically. Left behind now are the cool dim forests of fir, spruce and aspen. Now, away from the river, the flora is that of the cool, semi-arid climate of the Colorado Plateau. There is rabbit brush, chamisa, sage, silvery clumps of buffalo grass and the waving yellow cycles of grama grass. Then, as the valley opens, there are two-thirds of a million acres of farmland made fertile by the river itself.

This the first of the rich valleys through which the Rio Grande wanders. Most of them, like the river itself, are the product of a phenomenon of mind-boggling immensity. In terms of geological time it happened only yesterday—when many of America's other rivers had already been wearing away at their valleys for millions of years. Scientists can't time it exactly, but it came in the most recent era of the earth's formation—the Cenozoic—and in the age the geologists call the Miocene. The last of the dinosaurs had been extinct perhaps a hundred million years and the dominant life form of the continent was the mammal. We know only that 20 million years ago the Rio Grande didn't exist. About 15 million years ago it did. In that interim, the continental midlands underwent dramatic changes.

Here, a section of the earth's crust about 8,000 square miles in area began sinking. At the same time, the crust around it rose, forming the San Juan and Sangre de Cristo Mountains. The process was extremely slow but the results were impressive. An area a little larger than New Jersey was left as much as two miles lower than the land surrounding it. In the Albuquerque area, where this process still hasn't completely stabilized, the Sandia Mountains offer spectacular proof of the extent of this movement. To find the same strata of rocks that rim Sandia Crest almost 11,000 feet above sea level, one has to drill a little more than 6,500 feet below the bed of the Rio Grande that runs past the foot of the mountain. Thus in central New Mexico we know the vertical shift was more than two miles. In some places along the Rio Grande "graben" the gap is more than three miles.

At first these depressions were not connected. The mountains drained into them, forming huge inland seas. But time and gravity did their inevitable work. Millions of years of earthquakes, water erosion, glaciation and volcanic action gradually filled these lakes with stone, silt and ashes. The lake that once covered the San Luis Valley finally spilled over the great dam of volcanic basalt that had closed its southern end. It began cutting a channel, draining itself into the lake that covered the Española Valley below, causing it to overflow in turn. Thus the Rio Grande was born. Geologists believe the Rio Grande is a veritable infant among the continent's rivers—finally integrated to reach the Gulf of Mexico as late as 500,000 years ago.

At Alamosa on an autumn evening all this cosmic violence is hard to credit. Here alluvial fans have forced the river eastward, the towering San Juans have receded to ragged line on the western horizon and the Sangre de Cristos loom to the east. They are 30 miles distant, but in the luminous transparency of high, dry air they seem an easy walk away. A landscape as flat as Kansas wheat country stretches away in all directions. On this particular evening students from Adams State College are holding a picnic in the riverside park just inside the grassy old levee that protects the town from floods. Below the levee the river lies in long, still pools. The water seems dead, but the yellow leaves from the cottonwoods move on its surface—drawn inexorably southward. Between the voices of the students, there is the slightest suggestion of the music moving water makes. A family of muskrats make their home somewhere along this levee and one of them now swims slowly upstream on some chore—undismayed by collegiate laughter and my curiosity. Civilization has tamed him, as irrigation has tamed the river.

The first irrigation in the Upland Meadow does nothing more than water a few hundred acres, hardly affecting the stream. In the San Luis Valley, it's another matter. As the river reaches its junction with South Fork at the head of the valley, more than 1500 cubic-feet-per second of its water is diverted into the big Del Norte ditch. Before it reaches Lobatos Bridge at the bottom of the valley, the river feeds 70 other ditches. These arteries serve a sprawling network of capillaries that carry the Rio Grande miles from its bed to reach almost 700,000 otherwise arid acres. Before the Del Norte Ditch was built in 1882, the San Luis Valley was too dry to raise much more than cattle, hay and a few chancy crops of grain when it was unusually rainy. Now it produces an annual wealth of potatoes, sugar beets, cereals and vegetables. In its wandering 150-mile course through the valley, Rio Grande water is used again, and again, and again. The seepage from croplands is collected in drains, returned to the river, and diverted again to repeat the process. By the time it reaches the Colorado-New Mexico border, it is a tired, depleted river. But here it begins a new life and takes on a new character.

The San Luis Valley had been home only for nomadic Indians. The Stone Age hunters of the last Ice Age had come and gone. And then, thousands of years later, bands of Athabascan Indians moved into the park looking for the homeland they would call Dinetah and their destiny as the Navajo Nation. They were driven southward by fiercer people, Sioux and Cheyenne encroaching from the north, Comanches from the eastern Buffalo Plains and the Utes. The first recorded white expedition into the vast valley was drawn there in a counterattack against these raiders. A pugnacious Comanche war chief named Greenhorn (in recognition of the green

buffalo horn on his invincible helmet) was operating out of the valley to raid Indian pueblos and Spanish settlements downriver. Governor Juan de Anza of the Territory of New Mexico organized a mixed Spanish-Indian army of 600 men. He pursued the Comanches up the valley and over Poncha Pass. Greenhorn donned his magic helmet and was killed with a dozen of his warriors in the ensuing cavalry skirmish. The expedition told the Spanish that the source of the Rio Grande was the San Juan Mountains (and not somewhere near the North Pole as some had suspected) and left the immense valley of its source open for settlement. But the Spanish already had more land and Indian trouble in New Mexico than they could handle. Except for a few brave souls who moved into the lower end of the valley in the 19th Century, white settlement generally waited until the end of the Civil War brought rapid Western expansion of the United States. It wasn't until 1868 that the United States officially took the valley away from the Utes, opening it for homesteading and giving the tribe title a perpetual reservation in the San Juan mountains, which no one at the moment wanted. However, eternity proved brief for the Utes. Two years after the treaty was signed, prospectors searching for gold in violation of the agreement found a rich lode across Stony Pass. Miners poured in to develop the Silverton lode, the Stony Pass road was built to supply Silverton, and in 1873 the Utes were handed an amendment to their treaty in which they surrendered their rights to the San Juans. (Tribal survivors today are reduced to an arid, overgrazed patch of land in extreme southwestern Colorado.)

If you stand on the worn plank floor of the Lobatos Bridge just north of the New Mexico border, the only visible reminders of the tribes that once controlled the valley to the north are their sacred mountains. To the west, overlooking the Conejos River, is the cinder cone the maps call Ute Mountain, where the shamans of the tribe communed with their God. Directly upriver to the north looms Mount Blanca, one of the six sacred mountains of Navajo mythology. The Navajos call it Sis Naajini (White Shell Mountain). It was built by First Man and First Woman, who spread a blanket of white shell on the earth and piled upon it soil carried up from the dim, subterranean Third World. On top of this more white shell was spread and Dawn Boy, one of Holy People of the Navajos, entered the mountain to guard Dinetah (the Land of the People) from the East. Dawn Boy still lives there, watched over forever by Shash, the magic bear. But the People he was to guard are gone. The Rio Grande must pour through its great lava gorge into the Española Valley before it finds Indians who make it a part of their mythology and float the spirits of their dead upon its waters.

The line between the Rio Grande of the San Luis Valley and the Rio Grande below is appropriately abrupt and dramatic. It is formed by the Taos plateau—a layer of volcanic basalt and ash up to a quarter mile deep through which the river has sliced the great zigzag canyon called the Rio Grande Gorge.

Lobatos Bridge is at the very end of the San Luis. The flat croplands are gone now and the land beside the river rises in the gentle mounds—the time worn flanks of old, and minor, volcanic eruptions. It isn't flat enough here to irrigate, and too dry for trees—a sagebrush climate. The river lies in long, almost motionless pools in a shallow, gently sloping valley. The canyon develops a caprock rim only a few hundred yards above the bridge. As far as you can see downstream, this rim rises no more than 50 feet. But this is the beginning. At this lonely bridge that brotherhood which finds its thrills testing courage and skill against stone and fast water begin one of America's most challenging runs.

The American River Touring Association rates rivers on a scale similar to that used by mountain climbers to classify peaks and cliffs. The scale runs from an easy I to VI. The first 24 miles below Lobatos—from the bridge to Lee's Trail—is rated II. That means one with a rubber raft and "intermediate" experience can safely run it. Beyond Lee's Trail, the river becomes Class VI, which translates to "utmost difficulty—near limit of navigability"—a stretch of water that should be attempted only by a team of experts taking every precaution. Michael Jenkinson, author of *Wild Rivers of America,* calls the stretch between Lee's Trail and the point where Red River pours into the Rio Grande "pure nightmare." In that scant 12 miles, the river squanders 650 feet of it altitude. It's a thunderous passage, even at low water, with the river roaring through a convoluted series of chutes and rapids, breaking into plumes of spray on house-sized boulders, and slamming into the slick, black wall of its canyon. Experts have made it through this slot in low water seasons. But a team of professional river guides who tried it in the spring of 1970 gave up and climbed out after covering less than five miles in four dangerous and exhausting days.

In relation to the vast sweep of geologic history, the gorge is new, formed in the last half million years—the last tick of cosmic time. The river cut through this 50-mile volcanic block like a hot wire sinking into a cake of ice and not enough centuries have passed for wind, rain and gravity to soften the effect. The walls are sheer, the canyon narrow, and at places it is almost a thousand feet from rim to river.

For one approaching the Rio Grande across the Sunshine Valley north of Taos, this phenomenon can produce an eerie effect. Nothing on this great plateau suggests the nearness of a river. Sagebrush, chamisa, and grama grass stretch unbroken toward the western horizon. But as you near the rim of the still invisible gorge, you become aware of a sound. You seem to hear it through the soles of your feet—a muted subterranean thunder as if Mother Earth herself were murmuring in her eternal sleep. The sound, of course, is the booming of cataracts—tons of water pounding over basalt boulders.

Down among those water-slick boulders there is no surcease from sound. From Lee's Trail, about a dozen miles south of the Colorado border, to the confluence of the Red River, the Rio is a bedlam of boiling rapids. The fishermen who are lured into this noisy world can reach the upper end of this strip with a 220-foot descent from the rim. Twelve miles downstream at the La Junta campground, it takes a vertical climb of more than 800 feet to reach earth surface again. The trail is good, zigzagging safely up the cliff. But, safe or not, the effect is much like getting to the 80th floor of a skyscraper without using the elevator.

Among a small fraternity of fiercely ardent New Mexico and Colorado trout fishermen this sunken piece of river is known as "The Box." The pools they prefer are reached neither by Lee's nor La Junta trails. There are other ways down, rough and chancy, by which those agile, strong-lunged, brave and fanatic enough can lower themselves by dawn's light to a favorite pool and escape from the depth at sundown. The reward for this is a chance to catch German brown trout of trophy size (this piece of river is often called the best brown trout fishing in America), lunker rainbows, and, odd as it sounds, northern pike. The pike have appeared only recently. It's speculated that they made their way downstream from some Colorado lake and reproduced in the cold, oxygen-rich water of the deep canyon. There is another reward not measurable in pounds and inches. A day spent at the bottom is a day spent in a world which has nothing to do with civilization. The sun reaches the river only as it passes overhead at midday. The cliffs cut off everything, making the horizon a thin strip of blue overhead. The thunder of water echoes from the basalt walls and engulfs you. With all this there is the spicing of risk. The Rio Grande here demands respect. When the current is up, losing your footing on spray-slick stone can be lethal. Even a sprained ankle requires a complicated and time consuming team rescue effort. I recall four such rescue missions in the past five years (a drowned rafter, a dead fisherman, and two who survived). In a society which

has slain all its dragons, this noisy stretch of water serves a sort of primal purpose. The angler who emerges on the rim at sunset with the voice of the river shouting far below him tends to feel he has tested more than his fishing skill.

Below the mouth of Red River the Rio Grande briefly slows its pace. For the next ten miles the rapids rate only a Class III (challenging for those with intermediate experience). But at John Dunn Bridge, things change again. The bridge is the only water level access to the river for vehicles in 65 miles from Lobatos to Taos Junction. A road follows the Rio Hondo canyon from the village of Arroyo Hondo to the river and then climbs the cliff on the west side via awesome switchbacks. If rafters don't leave the river here they experience 17 miles of the loneliest and wildest water anywhere. The stretch is rated Class V, (exceptionally difficult for experts) and its Powerline Rapids, where rockslides divert the river against its wall, are called by Jenkinson "one of the toughest navigable rapids on this or any other river." On this lonely stretch the only signs a rafter will see that the planet is inhabited are the bottom of the Rio Grande Gorge Bridge (a structure so far overhead that it seems unreal) and the high voltage cable which gives the rapids its name.

U.S. 64 crosses the river on the high bridge at the midpoint of this 17 miles of wild water. Here, too, the lay of the sagebrush prairie makes the river invisible until the last moment. One second you are driving across a brushy flat; the next the roadside has disappeared and you, car, and highway are airborne. The span, supported on two pylons anchored on shoulders of the cliffs, soars 2,000 feet across the gorge and 800 above the river—it's the nation's second highest bridge. Here, air moving through the steel structure close at hand blends with the noise of water far below forming a duet of wind and river. It's one of few places I know of where one has a reasonable chance of looking down on the flight of golden eagle. These great predator birds nest in the canyon walls, and hunt rodents along the cliffs. Snowy egrets and great blue herons also sometime live in the canyon, and the mud cliff dwellings of swallows are everywhere on the lichen-stained canyon walls.

For the obvious reason that it offers the only water available for miles, less perpendicular portions of the gorge serve as a magnet for wildlife, including animals as large as mule deer and pronghorn antelope. Muskrats are plentiful, along with a few beaver, and the usual coyotes and bobcats there to prey on the small rodents. At Lee's Trail one can also witness the improbable sight of Hereford cattle in various stages of the laborious process of getting a drink of water. Some are at the canyon bottom, resting for the long ascent, some are making their way nervously down the narrow switchback path from the west rim, some are on the return trip, catching their breath at the elbows of zigzag turns. Since it is clearly impossible for two of the animals to pass at most places on the trail without tumbling one off the cliff, the Herefords have worked out a protocol for this daily ordeal. They rest only at wide places and begin ascents and descents in groups, thereby reducing the odds of confrontations.

The gorge ends 50 miles south of the Colorado border at the place where Taos Creek, a tiny clear stream at the bottom of an incredible canyon, trickles into the river. At this point, the river bottom widens into waterside benches, the cliffs are lower, and the Rio Grande undergoes another of its changes of character. By now there is more water. Costilla Creek has made its small donation just south of the New Mexico border, Rio Hondo and Red River have added their more considerable waters, and a series of springs deep in the gorge have made substantial contributions. The largest of these, Big Arsenic, pours 5,400 gallons per minute of pure, icy water out of a rockslide just upstream from La Junta trail. Thus revived, the Rio Grande enters its most historic territory —the Española Valley.

Ever since it emerged through Wagon Wheel Gap, the river

has been running through a land dotted with Spanish names: San Luis, Del Norte, Antonito, Lobatos, Conejos, Alamosa. But these are 19th Century places—settlements that in this river's span of history date back to only yesterday. Civilization in the middle valleys of the Rio Grande is immensely older.

Scientists believe that man first saw the Great River more than 20,000 years ago. The river was much larger then, carrying the melt water of the last glaciers and the runoff from the pluvial rains. In this cooler, wetter valley the Stone Age hunters we call Clovis and Folsom Man preyed on now-extinct longhorn bison, giant ground sloth, and the tiny camel and horses of that era. Perhaps 6,000 years ago, the climate along the river became much warmer and drier. Hunting—always a risky and marginal way of life—became impractical. Those who survived, shifted from a meat to a vegetable economy—subsisting on nuts, berries and what they could dig from the ground. Then, perhaps 2,000 years ago, corn appeared in the Rio Grande Valley.

Exactly where it came from, no one knows. Some of those whose civilizations flourished because of it have passed down the word of its origins in their myths. It was given them as a blessing from the gods. Among the Keresan-speaking pueblos along the river, corn was the final gift to them from *Latik*, the Mother of All, who helped them emerge from the underworld and who, before she left them, gave her people her heart, which was seed corn, and taught the tribal *caciques* the rules of life. Modern agronomists have sought in vain an explanation more scientific than this. Corn is a form of grass, but because of the way its seeds are tightly secured on a cob, it won't reproduce without the help of human cultivation. Therefore it could not, so it seems, evolve naturally.

However it evolved, corn made a food surplus, a sedentary agricultural life, and civilization possible along middle valleys of the great river. The first known communal settlement was about 250 A.D., at the Artificial Lake Site near what is now downtown Albuquerque. As early as 600 A.D., the art of pottery making was widespread and the people who were to become the Pueblo Indians were developing a sophisticated social community and a complex architecture. By the year 1,000, when Europeans were suffering through the bloody savagery we call the Dark Ages, these people had flowered into one of the most humane, peaceful, and democratic societies the world has ever known. This Golden Age of the pueblos produced the great communal dwellings of Mesa Verde, Chaco Canyon, Frijoles Canyon, and elsewhere—some abandoned during an epic cycle of drought in the 12th Century, and some abandoned for reasons which remain a total mystery. Whatever the cause, the people moved away from the cliffs and plateaus closer to the Rio Grande, which they called T'sina, or Kanyapakwa, or P'osoge—depending on whether their language was Tewa, or Towa, or Keresan. (Whatever the language, the name translates to something close to "great river.") They included it in the mythology of their wanderings, and built diversion dams of stone where its banks were low, and chopped out ditches to lead its water into their fields of corn, beans and squash. And when Europeans finally came to this part of the Rio Grande, they found more than 60 of these peaceful little city-states flourishing in the middle valley.

It has been said before that the Pueblo civilization was fortunate that the Europeans were not the English—who with a stolid lack of malice would soon be exterminating the woodland tribes along the Eastern seaboard. They were also fortunate that the Spanish came late. The mouth of the river had been discovered by Piñeda's little fleet in 1519. Cortez was in the Valley of Mexico prior to that year fighting Aztecs, and the brothers Pizarro were still 13 years away from their conquest of Peru. But almost 80 years passed before the Spanish finally found time to convert the discovery into colonization—and in those 80 years history worked in complicated ways. The river was destined to see a different generation of conquistadores. The climate of the times had changed and with it some of the fierce, cruel, self-confident arrogance had mellowed out of the cutting edge of Spanish empire. When the Spanish finally came to the middle river to stay, the moody, deeply religious Philip II had replaced Charles V on the throne of Spain. Pope Leo X had died. The Catholic theologians had declared that the natives of the New World were humans, exactly as the Spanish. The Indians were the sons of God. The Good News of Christianity must be preached to them so that they might become beloved subjects of the Two Majesties—the cross and the crown. Instead of Cortez, the gentle Pueblo cities received Don Juan de Oñate—and survived with their culture intact.

But it was a narrow escape.

Piñeda had been impressed with what he had seen at the mouth of this river—a flat mild land forested with coconut palms. The river was muddy but deep, meandering through a vast delta. The people were uncivilized and poor, with no sign of agriculture. But they were friendly enough, providing the Spanish with shellfish, nuts and berries in exchange for cloth and bells. The river must lead toward the Pacific Ocean, which Balboa had discovered just six years before. Piñeda called it the River of Palms and recommended to his *jefe*, Governor Garay of Jamaica, that a settlement be founded without delay. The following year, Diego de Camargo arrived with a small fleet to establish a town in Garay's name. He picked a site upstream from what is now Port Isabel, began building a fort, alienated the Indians, and escaped to sea after a wild ship-versus-canoe battle down 20 miles of river. In 1522, Garay himself came with a stronger force, but changed his mind and decided, instead, to contest Cortez for control of the Panuco River territory to the south. That ended Garay. Next, the notorious Nuño de Guzmán and Panfilo de Narváez were both given jurisdiction over the Rio Grande in overlapping grants from the Crown. Guzmán's plans for a colony came to nothing. Narváez, who also planned a settlement, produced instead a spectacular, epic disaster which would finally affect the pueblos—1,000 miles upstream.

Narváez, faced with storms in the Gulf, landed his expedition on the west coast of Florida and sent his fleet westward. But the ships were lost and the army disintegrated. Only five men are known to have survived of the 400 landed. Four of them reached Mexico City in 1536 after seven years and some 3,000 miles of wandering. They had reached the Rio Grande at about the present site of El Paso. The Indians there lived in dugouts and thatched huts and were poor to the point of starvation. The four wanderers had lived with them for months, and listened to stories of a rich civilization up the river where the Indians lived in multistoried cities and used gemstones for arrowheads. One of the survivors was Nuñez Cabeza de Vaca, Royal Treasurer of the Narváez colony and a man to be believed. Among ambitious men in Mexico City, the tales of Cabeza de Vaca spread and grew. In 1539, Francisco Vásquez de Coronado sent another of the survivors—a Negro named Estebanico—and a Franciscan priest named Friar Marcus de Niza to explore. Estebanico was killed at one of the Zuni pueblos, but Friar Marcus returned and reported what he had seen and heard. He had seen villages of puddled adobe, and fields of corn, and a terraced town of stone, but he had heard of Cíbola, which the Indians told him consisted of seven cities—their streets paved with turquoise and their people decorated with golden ornaments. In 1540, twenty-one years after Piñeda's discovery, Coronado launched his famous expedition to find Cíbola and find out what lay up the Great River of the North.

It might be said that Coronado fell somewhere between Oñate and Cortez in nature as well as historic time. He took the Zuñi pueblos by storm, killing 20 warriors, but treated the survivors humanely. When the pueblos the Spanish called Arenal and Moho revolted, Arenal and most of its defenders were burned. But during the 50-day siege of Moho, Coronado arranged the safe evacuation of women and children when the pueblo's water supply was exhausted. And when the defense finally collapsed, the Indian wounded received medical care and the prisoners were released. Coronado was explorer and not settler. He probed a thousand miles into the buffalo plains seeking the illusion of Quivira, a sort of golden Oz of the grass country. His lieutenants probed up the river as far as Taos Pueblo and down the river to the vicinity of El Paso. (There in late summer they saw one of the characteristics of the Rio Grande which still surprises Easterners. They reported the river vanished under its sandy bed, only to surface again far downstream.) In 1542, Coronado withdrew his army from the river and went home to Mexico to die. His expensive failure thoroughly disillusioned the Spanish, and the river flowed in peace for another 40 years.

The great and fundamental change began for the middle valley in 1598. On April 20, Don Juan de Oñate arrived at the River of the North, and with him came 130 families, 270 soldiers, 11 Franciscan priests, and 7,000 head of livestock. Oñate was to be Royal Governor of a new colony and extend effective control by the Spanish Empire almost a thousand miles northward. The people with him came to stay, and stay they did. After almost 400 years their family names are still the place names of the river country.

Oñate had reached the river several miles downstream from the present site of El Paso. He had abandoned the old roundabout route to the Rio Grande, which followed up the valley of the Rio Conchos to Junta de los Rios, and explored a shorter and more direct passage. His route became known as the Camino Real, the Royal Road that would for two and a half centuries be the only artery connecting Mexico City with the river colony. While shorter, it was still a hideously difficult 2,000-mile trek across the Sonoran Desert. For 250 years the Rio Grande colony would suffer from extreme isolation from military and economic support.

Before he moved his party upriver, Oñate celebrated his arrival with a solemn high Mass at an altar under the cottonwoods, and a fiesta at which a play was presented. It dramatized the conversion of the Indians to Christianity by the Franciscan friars. It was a prophetic performance. By September, with his capital established across the river from the pueblo he named San Juan, Oñate invited leaders of all pueblos to a meeting. Thirty-two were represented at the session. The caciques were asked first to swear allegiance to the new government. They agreed to do so. They were then told of Christianity by Friar Alonzo Martínez, one of the Franciscans, and asked to accept the new faith. After a discussion among themselves the Indian spokesman said they would like to learn about it, but the bargain would be that they would become Christians only if they liked what they were taught. And so it started. Each of the priests was assigned to a group of pueblos, and departed alone with the Indians to found his new parish. Thus began an abiding relationship between the complex humanistic faith of the Pueblos and the equally complex Catholic faith. As taught by the Franciscans of that period—with their emphasis on brotherly love, human interdependence, and rejection of materialism—Catholicism had much in common with Pueblo values. The Indians, too, believed in a single Creator, in a benevolent mother-figure, in a personal soul that lived after death of the body, and their kachina spirits were very similar to the Catholic belief in the "community of saints." (Among the Navajos, Apaches and Comanches, with a totally different set of beliefs and values, the Franciscan missionaries had virtually no success.)

The alliance was not without its strains. Acoma had been represented at the San Juan meeting only by observers. That winter, 11 members of a patrol visiting the pueblo were killed in a surprise attack. Oñate attacked the mesa-top stronghold, captured it after an epic battle, and sentenced all male prisoners over 25 years old to have one foot amputated. Friction also developed quickly between the Franciscans, who accused the military government of misusing the Indians, and the military, who accused the Franciscans of coddling their charges. The first period of colonization along the river was marked by increasing bitterness between church and state with the Pueblo Indian most often the subject of the quarrel. Governors were excommunicated, priests arrested. Theoretically the argument had been settled in 1537, when Pope Paul III had issued a strongly worded Papal Bull. Satan himself, said the Pope, inspired those Spaniards who declared that Indians should be treated "as dumb brutes created for our service, pretending that they are incapable of receiving the Catholic Faith." The Pope declared that these Indians were not to be deprived of their possessions, or their liberty, even if they did not accept Christianity.

In 1613, just three years after Oñate had moved his capital from near San Juan to the new Royal City of the Holy Faith (Santa Fe), Friar Isidro Ordóñez refused to let Indians of the Taos Pueblo deliver a levy of corn to tax collectors sent by Governor Pedro de Peralta. The governor sent troops and collected the corn anyway. Ordóñez denounced the governor for using press gangs of Indians to build the Palace of Governors at Santa Fe (they built well; after 365 years it is still in use) and excommunicated Peralta. Peralta fired his pistol at the priest, but missed.

Peralta and Ordóñez were replaced, but the conflict continued. It bore bitter fruit.

There were, as there had always been, years of drought and famine. But now the balance of human ecology had changed. The Mescalero Apaches of the mountains, and the Kiowa-Comanches of the plains now had horses. Hungry, they raided the pueblos with increasing effectiveness and ferocity. The Spanish population by 1670 numbered no more than 2,500. It could spare an average of no more than four soldiers to guard a pueblo. The so-called Saline pueblos east of the river were abandoned and left to fall to ruins. The Apaches struck at the major river pueblo of Senecu, killed its priest and half its inhabitants. It, too, was abandoned. In the face of this murderous external threat, the Spanish continued their own church-versus-state battle over the treatment of their Indian allies. Then in 1680, the pueblos took a hand of their own in this dispute.

The revolution was planned at Taos, led by a cacique named Po-pe. On August 10, the northern pueblos struck in unison—killing the local Spanish and then marching into Santa Fe. Governor Antonio de Otermín and the survivors he could rally held out in the Palace of Governors, and then broke out and fought their way downriver to El Paso, collecting survivors on the way. By autumn the Spanish colony upriver had ceased to exist.

The reconquest came in 1692. The remarkable Don Diego de Vargas led a small army upriver. He found the Indian alliance had collapsed, and with much bluff and diplomacy, reoccupied Santa Fe and obtained the submission of 22 pueblos without losing a soldier or killing an Indian. What Otermín had called "the miserable kingdom" was restored. It would survive, in hunger and hardship and constant warfare with Comanche, Apache and Navajo, until taken by the United States in 1848.

Downriver, the effect of the Europeans was slower in coming. The Franciscans founded a mission at the much-used ford we now call El Paso in 1659. In 1699, Fort John the Baptist and three missions were built at the ford called France Way, 300 crow-flight miles from the river mouth. San Antonio and a few other small settlements were founded north of the river in the 18th Century. But the lower river saw little change until the 1820s. In 1821 the flag of Spain came down all along the Rio Grande and was replaced by the banner of an independent Mexico. The same year immigrant colonies of Anglo-Americans were founded in the trans-river territory of Texas.

The Spanish government had given a foiled St. Louis banker named Moses Austin permission to settle 300 families in Texas. The new Mexican government, preoccupied by its civil war, let the approval stand. It proved to be a fateful decision. That year, 302 years after discovery, there were fewer than 3,000 Spanish (now Mexicans) in all of the vast province of the lower Rio Grande. In less than 10 years, Moses' sickly son, Stephen, had moved in some 5,600 Anglo-Americans—almost all slaveholding families from Louisiana and other Southern states.

One of the first acts of the Mexican government was to outlaw slavery. In the Coahuila-Texas territory, straddling the Rio Grande, the outraged Texas slaveholders managed first to win an exemption from the decree, and then to have it modified to cover only those born six months after passage of the act. There were other causes of friction, ranging from custom fees to (incredible as it seems in an immense, almost empty country) trouble over land ownership between Mexican settlers and immigrants from the U.S. The immigrants proclaimed an independent Republic of Texas, and in the winter of 1833 the Rio Grande saw General Antonio Lopez de Santa Ana, President of Mexico and commander of its army, ferry 6,000 troops across to put an end to this treason. Santa Ana wiped out a rebel force defending the Alamo at San Antonio, and won another victory at Goliad. In both places he ordered his reluctant officers to kill all prisoners. Then, at San Jacinto Creek, the Mexican army was routed and Santa Ana captured. The hostage president signed a treaty granting Texas its independence.

That same year, a quieter revolution happened in the old province of Nuevo Mexico. The Franciscan Order, which had been heart and soul of Spanish-Pueblo alliance and source of most of the education upriver, was withdrawn. Secular priests, in theory, replaced the friars. In fact, there were virtually no secular priests, and no financial support to replace the subsidy which had come for generations from the great world-wide Franciscan Order. Within a few years, the churches in many towns, and in most of the pueblos, were standing empty and falling into ruin. Upriver, too, the outside world had been intruding into the isolated Spanish colony. Lieutenant Zebulon Pike had crossed the Front Range of the Rockies in 1808 and camped on the Rio Grande near the mouth of the Conejos. (He pretended when a Spanish patrol came to inquire that he thought it was the Red River.) Pike was escorted downriver to Santa Fe, and eventually to Chihuahua, and then back to Fort John the Baptist to be expelled from the Spanish Territory. He took with him information that in the United States removed the mystery from the Mountain West and the Rio Grande. After Pike, the insatiable Yankee appetite for trade, and a European fad which made hats of beaver fur immensely popular, brought a steady increase in the intrusion of Anglo-Americans into the Spanish-Indian world upriver. The Santa Fe Trail opened, linking Santa Fe with U.S. markets over a road that, while 800 miles long, was much easier and quicker than old Royal Road across mountains and deserts to Mexico City. And the demand for fur brought hundreds of French and Anglo-American trappers swarming into the mountains that rim the river's upper basin. In the 30 years before Chinese silk killed the fur trade, these mountain men made legends in the high country of the San Juans and the Sangre de Cristos. By the late 1820s they were bringing 40,000 pounds of pelts, worth $5 a pound, out of the mountains each spring. They exterminated the grizzly bear and challenged the mountain Indians for dominion of their territory. When the price of beaver skidded, many remained and added a new element to the culture upriver.

The final great political change came in 1846-48—affecting the river all along its 1,900 miles. The United States annexed the Republic of Texas, war with Mexico flared, and the defeated Santa Ana signed the Treaty of Guadalupe Hidalgo, recognizing the independence of Texas and ceding to the United States its upriver territory and the land from the Gila River to the 42nd parallel and from the Pacific to Rio Grande. The flag of the United States waved now all along the river. Except for one month in the Civil War era, when Texas joined the Confederacy and carried the Stars and Bars upstream as far as Santa Fe, it would remain. And it would bring to the Great River the overwhelming forces of American civilization—railroads, industrial development, and a flood of immigration. The uneasy joint dominion of Indian tribe and Spanish outpost along the river was ended. The power of the Comanche, Kiowa, Ute, Pawnee, Navajo and Apache was gradually crushed. And the river itself was measured, allocated, and adjudicated, and—most important—controlled.

The water that pours out of the narrow mouth of the Rio Grande Gorge under the old Taos Junction Bridge has been predicted and allocated long before the snow which produced it melted. It has been gauged repeatedly on its route down the mountain streams and through the myriad irrigation ditches of the San Luis Valley. Under the Lobatos Bridge the pulse of the Rio Grande is taken to determine if Colorado farmers used more than their share of the last winter's snow. When it reaches Otowi Gauge halfway through New Mexico, its volume is gauged again. On a "normal" year, when about a million acre feet of water run under Otowi Bridge, 53 percent must be delivered into Elephant Butte Reservoir for use in the Juarez-El Paso Valley of Texas-Mexico and in the Mesilla Valley of New Mexico. What these, and other gauges report determines whether water must be released, or retained in reservoirs on the tributary streams that feed the great river. In much of the immense Colorado-New Mexico basin, no dams over 10 feet high can be built, no water wells drilled, without permission of the State Engineer. The right to use water from the river, or the streams that flow into the river, or the moist sands that are supplied by water seeping toward the river, is a valuable property to be bought and sold. It is carefully guarded, and exactly graded—generally on the basis of chronological use. Since the Pueblo Indians were using irrigation water when the Spanish arrived, and their rights were recognized by Spanish law, the Pueblos generally have the senior rights and top priorities. Next come those who hold rights on the old Spanish-colonial ditches. (The Chamita ditch has been irrigating fields since 1724.) On each stream "priorities" are based on location and availability of the ditch to water. And even the individual ditches have their own priorities—the value of each determined by location.

Oddly, where irrigation is oldest on the river it is least important in terms of dollars. The first diversion in the canyon is at Pilar, where the stream is tapped to water the few acres of orchards and vegetable gardens of the old village. Here the canyon widens enough to accommodate U.S. 64-86, and the pavement runs on the bench above the water for 30 miles. The next diversion comes at Velarde, again to water a few hundred acres of apples, peaches, cherries, plums and fields of chili. At Velarde, the canyon widens toward the Española Valley. Here is the oldest center of civilization in the United States. Each of the little tributary streams that drain the Sangre de Cristo Mountains (named for the "Blood of Christ") is the site of its Spanish colonial village. There is Trampas, Truchas, Santa Cruz, Chimayo, Cundiyo, Cordova, Alcalde, Embudo and the rest. Most of them were old when George Washington was a boy. They remain, much as they always were—poor adobe buildings, clustered around an adobe church, occupied by families whose names appeared on the roster of Oñate, or of De Vargas. The river itself passes by even older habitations—the pueblo of San Juan, still about the size it was when Oñate established his capital just across the river, and just below the confluence of the Chama, the equally ancient pueblos of Santa Cruz and San Ildefonso.

The Chama is the last of the Rio Grande's major tributaries until the Rio Conchos, almost a thousand miles downstream.

Since 1968, part of the contribution it makes to the Great River is water which nature intended for the Colorado River and the Pacific Ocean. It has been diverted from the watershed of the San Juan River via a tunnel bored through the Continental Divide. It is dumped into Willow Creek to flow into Heron Reservoir and hence into the Chama. It flows clear, cold and aswarm with rainbow trout, into the flood control reservoir behind El Vado Dam, and downstream into the flood control dam at Abiquiu, and through the Chama Valley. By now it has dissolved tons of soft, yellow deposits and become a sort of muddy orange.

From the San Luis Valley outlet through the Española Valley, the Rio Grande drops from 7,440 feet to 5,600. Much of this altitude is lost in the precipitous descent through the gorge. But the canyon from Taos Junction past Pilar to Velarde, and all the way to the Chama, offers boating opportunities which, if less exciting than the gorge, are much more convenient. From the bridge to Pilar a good dirt road follows the east bank of the river and the entire strip is a New Mexico state park with picnic and camping facilities. At Pilar the river drops down a five-mile stretch of rapids which are rated an expert Class IV. Near the old wooden Woody Glen Bridge, the Great River is pinched into a narrows (only five feet wide at one point) providing a test of nerve for kayak operators. The fast water ends at the village of Rinconada and for the next 30 miles one can drift effortlessly through the Española Valley, past cottonwood bosques and Indian pueblos and a patchwork of orchards and vegetable gardens.

The next white water run comes at the end of the valley. The river passes under Otowi Bridge into White Rock Canyon. For 25 miles it will wind its way through a narrow cut between the Pajarito and Santa Fe plateaus. It loses about 10 feet per mile, which makes for fast water, and its rapids are rated difficult for experienced boaters even at low water.

The scenery here is spectacular—eroded cliffs in which white volcanic pumice is layered with streams of lava. Here Frijoles Creek drains into the river. Up this little stream are the Frijoles cliff dwellings, where ancestors of the present pueblo dwellers lived from the 1200s to about 1550. Why they abandoned the site remains one of anthropology's more baffling mysteries.

At the bottom of the canyon the river pours into Cochiti Reservoir—a massive earth-fill structure completed in 1975 to provide flood and sedimentation control (and a 50,000-acre-foot recreation lake) for the Middle Rio Grande Valley. When filled, the lake will bury most of the rapids of White Rock Canyon—backing water almost to Otowi Bridge.

Downstream from the new dam, the Rio Grande once again becomes a working river. This is the territory of the Keresan-speaking Pueblos, and the river irrigates the fields of the Cochití, Santo Domingo and San Felipe Indians, and pours past the old villages of Algodones and Bernalillo to Albuquerque.

In New Mexico's largest urban area (about 300,000 in Greater Albuquerque in the mid-1970s) the Rio Grande manages to affect the city without being affected. It wanders between a high bluff on its west bank and a levee on the east over a broad, sandy bed lined with cottonwoods. It is guarded from population by irrigation ditches and drains that parallel its bed, and insulated from urban affairs by broad belt of shady bosque. Within a few blocks of the city's downtown business district it provides a strip of natural shady silence still wild enough to attract migrating waterfowl.

The nature of this Middle Rio Grande can best be seen and understood from the crest of Sandia Mountain, which overshadows the river at Albuquerque. From this 11,000-foot ridge, the river is a streak of silver, running through a belt of pale green (gold in autumn, grey in winter) winding through a brown-grey, semidesert landscape. In the Española Valley, the mountains crowd the river—Sangre de Cristos to the east, and Jemez to the west. Here the western mountains have

receded—replaced by the great grassy hump called the plain of Albuquerque. But all through New Mexico and into Texas, mountains dominate the river landscape. Below Albuquerque the great high plain on the west is soon replaced by the Ladron Mountains, the Gallinas, the San Mateos, and, finally, the great Black Range, the Mimbres, and the barren Sierra de Uvas, which look down on the Mesilla Valley. To the east the mountain wall is equally ubiquitous. The Sandias give way to the Manzanos, which fade away into the Sierra Oscura and become the 100-mile-long ridge of the San Andres Mountains.

The Rio Grande meanders down this interwoven trough, its banks shaded by broad cottonwoods, tamarisk and willows and its water depleted to irrigate thousands of small farms that make up the Middle Rio Grande Irrigation District. At Socorro, some 80 miles south of Albuquerque, the basin narrows into the San Marcial marshes. Away from the river, the landscape is what the botanist call Upper Sonoran Desert—the eroded flanks of the hills covered with an infinity of dark green creosote bush and the grey-white desert grasses. Nature, with some help from the U.S. Fish and Wildlife service, has made this stretch of the Rio Grande a wilderness for birds.

It's called the Bosque del Apache Wildlife refuge (after the Apaches who used the riverside expanse of cottonwood forest as a staging area for raids upriver). In winter it is home for thousands of snow geese, Canada geese, greater sandhill cranes, clouds of ducks and other waterfowl, and a multitude of other birds in dazzling varieties. At these marshes, the old Royal Road was forced away from the river. For 90 almost waterless miles the old road ran east of a range of low, barren hills on a route the Spanish called Jornada del Muerte (Dead Man's Route). Oñate's colonists blazed this trail, and might have perished on it had not the Tiguex Pueblos sent food to help them.

Out of these narrow marshes the Rio Grande pours into Elephant Butte Reservoir, a 40-mile-long holding basin that waters the rich Mesilla Valley. When completed in 1916, this lake would hold 2,639,000 acre feet of water. Silting has reduced this capacity, and the Bureau of Reclamation once estimated that by 2016 the huge lake would be filled with topsoil washed downstream. The Cochiti Dam, and other flood control dams on upstream tributaries are now slowing this process. They are also easing the silting problem at Albuquerque, where the bed of the river (behind its levee) is as much as seven feet higher than nearby city streets.

From Elephant Butte, the Rio Grande is released into the Caballo Lake holding basin, and hence downriver into the network of canals that water one of the most productive expanses of cropland. The river waters 150,000 acres in New Mexico, another 80,000 acres in the El Paso valley of Texas, and 52,000 acres in the adjoining Juarez irrigation district of Mexico. The Elephant Butte district is one of the nation's major sources of long-staple cotton (more than 100,000 tons in a good year) and produces other crops, ranging from lettuce and onions to pecans and goose down.

At El Paso, the river simultaneously begins its thousand-mile role as international boundary and passes through its largest urban district—separating the industrial cities of El Paso and Juarez, Mexico. It is dirty here, polluted by use and reuse through hundreds of miles of ditches and drains, and confined to a concrete channel. Before its wandering ways were thus curbed, it had changed its course, and cut the Chamisal district of Juarez off from Mexico—causing years of international friction. Today, the river runs properly north of Chamisal, and Mexico has converted its recovered territory into an eye-catching park-monument to a friendly border.

The border has not always been friendly. South of the river lies the state of Chihuahua, the "Mother of Revolutions" in a nation that spent much of its first century engaged in internal strife. Benito Juarez used the Mexican city south of the river (then called El Paso del Norte) as the base of his crusade to free his country from Spanish rule, and to liberate it from the French who replaced the Spanish. Both Francisco Madero and Pancho Villa used it as a base again in the social revolution that gave Mexico its modern republican constitution. The city has been beseiged, burned and captured, and more than once bullets have crossed the river to make the streets of El Paso dangerous.

For generations, El Paso streets were made dangerous enough by their own inhabitants. The Treaty of Guadalupe Hidalgo split the little settlement on the river ford into U.S. and Mexican towns and made both sides a convenient hang-out for fugitives. When it was incorporated in 1873, El Paso had a total population of 173 citizens. But the Southern Pacific, Santa Fe, Texas Pacific and the Mexican Central rail-roads all connected into the community in 1881 and 1882, restoring its role as international crossroads and bringing it a flood of citizens (including John Wesley Hardin, whom legend credits with killing 26 men—six more than Billy the Kid) and a widespread reputation as gambling and sin center of the Southwest. In 1910, the city prohibited gambling and dance halls and since the 1920s, its economy has been based on agriculture, ore smelting, international trade and Fort Bliss, the base from which the United States Army trains anti-air-craft and artillery missile personnel on desert test ranges that extend some 200 miles in New Mexico.

Perhaps no place along its 1,900 miles has the Rio Grande been so altered by man as at this famous crossing. Its length has been cut by concrete channels that reduce 150 miles of meandering bends to less than 90 miles. The river, which had been described as "a mile wide, a foot deep, too thin to plow and too thick to drink, always flooding, and always changing beds," now passes through the El Paso-Juarez corridor as orderly and predictable as plumbing.

But here the Rio Grande, as we have seen it from its source at Stony Pass, has about played out its string. At Fort Quitman, the El Paso-Juarez Valley narrows and the last irrigation drain trickles what remains of its water back into the river. As far as those who manage the Rio Grande Interstate Compact are concerned, the river that drains the Southern Rockies is fin-ished. It has come almost 700 miles and irrigated almost a million acres, and used up more than 9,000 feet of altitude. At Fort Quitman, the river is only 3,400 feet above sea level, with 1,200 miles still to travel before it reaches the Gulf.

For the next hundred miles, the depleted Rio Grande runs through the narrow, desert valley between the barren Quit-man Mountains of Texas and Chihuahua's waterless Sierra del Huesco. On the U.S. side, the highway quits the river country at Fort Hancock. On the Mexican side, the farm road that has wandered down through a rosary of bosque villages (San Augustin, Guadalupe, Bravos, San Ignacio, Nuevo, and Cedillos) fades to nothing at Banderas. Along the river there are a few desert willows and tamarisk. Otherwise it is a dead landscape of stone and cactus—uninhabited on both sides of the border for almost 100 miles. Only reptiles live in this landscape—and those few mammals that—like the kangaroo rat—can live without drinking. And then, just above the place where an international bridge links Presidio, Texas, with the ancient adobe town of Ojinaga, Mexico, the Rio Conchos appears, like a miracle out of the stony desert, and pours a transfusion of cold, clear water into the Rio Grande.

The Franciscan, Fray Agustín Rodríguez, found this place in 1581 while exploring for souls to save. Finding a few Indians here, the Mission del Apostól Santiago was built to convert them—and later the Presidio to protect the mission from Comanches. Forty miles below this historic "Junta del Rios," the revived Great River squanders much of what alti-tude is left to it, roaring through three of America's most spectacular canyons. Here, sometime in the Cenozoic era, a series of geologic paroxysms bent and folded the earth crust and produced a ragged cluster of mountains, the Sierra del

Consuelo, the Sierra Carmen in Mexico and the Chisos in Texas. Through them, the river is forced southward into "The Big Bend" and through the awesome, twisting slots called Santa Elena, Mariscal and Boquillas Canyons.

As in the Rio Grande gorge, the river here is walled by immense, vertical cliffs, but the Big Bend canyons are very different from the gorge. The river below Lobatos bridge seems to sink into a black lava earth. Here, below the ford at the village of Lajitas, the earth seems to rise skyward around the river. At the upper end of Santa Elena Canyon, the river slides silently toward the immense limestone upthrust of Mesa de Anguila, which rises almost 1,800 feet above water level. The river flows through a slot in this formation. A mile inside it encounters the Big Bend country's most dangerous rapids, the "Rockslide." The Rio Grande pours through a jumble of great polished boulders and is considered lethal, even for the experts, in high water. Much of the float through all three canyons, however, is relatively easy at lower water, and much different from the black gorge in New Mexico. Here, cliffs and boulders are more often limestone white than basalt black, the canyon is generally much wider at the bot-tom, the cliffs higher and more vertical, the water warm and murky instead of cold and clear, and the endless thunder of the gorge rapids replaced by an eerie silence. And, instead of a continuous cut of 50 miles, the Big Bend canyons are sep-arated by open country. Marisal Canyon is almost 50 miles of open desert below Santa Elena and, like Santa Elena, a narrow, twisting slot walled in by limestone cliffs. They rise, like sky-scrapers from a street, from 1,500 to 1,800 feet.

For a hundred miles east of the Big Bend country, the river passes through empty desert—past the treeless, waterless ridges of the Sierra del Carmen and the margin of the vast Edwards Plateau. Before it reaches the communities of Del Rio and Ciudad Acuña where it is joined in the Amistad Res-ervoir by the Pecos and the Devils rivers, the Rio Grande has gone through almost 300 miles of isolation, unbridged and, except for Big Bend Park roads, difficult to reach. Now its character changes again. It slides past the hill country of Texas and, for the first time since Fort Quitman, it irrigates a rich valley. The land flattens, and the climate subtly changes. At Del Rio, the river bed is only 950 feet above sea level. Where it flows under the bridge linking Laredo and Nuevo Laredo it has 440 feet of altitude left. The countryside here is flat—cactus and mesquite country were not reclaimed by irrigation canals. The Gulf of Mexico is still 350 miles downstream but its climate is already affecting the river.

There is humidity in the air now, and a sense of mildness. The cycle of the river is also changed. Its heavy runoff season has shifted from the spring of mountain snowmelts to the late-summer and autumn of Gulf Coast rainstorms.

The largest reservoir on the river, a 3,000,000-acre-foot lake behind the Falcon Dam, controls the final 150 miles of the river and waters one of the richest river deltas this side of the Nile. Falcon Lake is also fed by the Rio Salado and Rio Sabinas and provides steady diet of water for almost a million acres of citrus groves and cropland on both sides of the bor-der. The river is bigger here. It was on this strip that Captain Henry Austin's steamship "Ariel" hauled cargo and passen-gers for his cousin's new colony in the 1820s. (Austin could take his paddlewheeler as far west as Roma even at low water.) It is still, in many places, lined by the palms for which Piñeda named it. But here it has run out of altitude. Much of its irrigation water is lifted from its ditches by pumps. It flows past Rio Grande City, Mission, Reynosa and finally under the bridges that link Brownsville with that historic gateway-to-Mexico, Matamoros. It is now a tropical river, a tidewater river. As the seabirds fly, it is only 30 miles to the Gulf of Mexico. But through this pool-table flatness the Rio Grande wanders a hundred miles before it finally delivers its muddy surplus to the sea.

Ice crystals on Squaw Creek, upper Rio Grande primitive area, Colorado

Ice sheets on the upper Rio Grande

Pinos Creek, Colorado □ Simpson Mountain, San Juan Mountains, Colorado

South Fork of the Rio Grande

Finger Mesa; San Juan Mountains, Colorado

Mountains at River Hill, upper river

Aspen trees, San Juan Mountains

Beaver dam at Thirty Mile Campground

Rio Grande Pyramid, San Juan Mountains

Mountain meadows near Clear Creek. Right: Cottonwood trees at Wagon Wheel Gap

Upper river area at Seven Mile. Left: Mine structure at Creede, Colorado

San Luis Valley, Colorado

Alkali covered prairie, Alamosa National Wildlife Refuge

Rubber raft running a Rio Grande gorge □ Sangre De Cristo Mountains from Lobatos Bridge Colorado

Siphon tube irrigating barley fields, Alamosa, Colorado

San Luis Valley, Colorado

San Antonio Peak, New Mexico. Right: Rio Grande Gorge, near Questa, New Mexico

Basalt cliff at Arroyo Hondo, New Mexico. Juniper on river gorge, Cebolla Mesa

Mission at Ranches of Taos

Indian Paintbrush above the canyon wall, Rio Grande Gorge

Puye Cliff dwellings, New Mexico

River gorge above Rio Grande Gorge Bridge

Prairie at Questa looking over the gorge

Sheep on a ranch at Arroyo Seco, New Mexico

Ruins of the prehistoric dwellers of Frijoles Canyon □ High mesa at Bandelier National Monument

Ancient dwellings at Bandelier

Ancient Indian trails, Tsankawi Section, Bandelier

Ponderosa pine in Frijoles Canyon

River bank in White Rock Canyon

Reconstructed kiva painting, Coronado State Monument, Bernalillo, New Mexico

Sandia Mountains, New Mexico

Snow covered mesa near San Ysidro

Above Mesa De Loro west of Albuquerque

St. Augustine church, Isleta Pueblo, New Mexico

Pueblo Indian designs, Petroglyph State Park, Albuquerque

Drying corn, Acoma Indian Reservation

Ceramic pot, Acoma Indian Reservation

The sky city, Acoma Pueblo

74

Decorative beam in an adobe, Acoma □ Late sun over the Black Range, New Mexico

Maple in the Sandia Mountains

Sandia Mountains, New Mexico

Windmill in the Magdalena Mountains

Organ Mountains east of Las Cruces, New Mexico

Ox cart, San Elizario Museum, San Elizario, Texas

Mesquite tree, Candelaria, Texas

Yucca in sand dunes, Hudspeth County, Texas

San Elizario, Mission, Texas

Ranchero, Ojinaga, Mexico

Rio Concho, Chihulahua, Mexico □ Sierra Del Carmen, from Big Bend National Park, Texas

Old stone mine ruins near Terlingua, Texas

Prickley poppy □ Rio Grande at Boquillas, Mexico

Dried yucca, Big Bend National Park, Texas

Painted Desert, Big Bend National Park

Giant dagger yucca, Big Bend National Park

Ferryboat to Santa Elena, Mexico

Ocotillo in bloom

Santa Elena Canyon, Big Bend National Park

Santa Elena Canyon, Big Bend National Park

Prickly pear cactus

Deer, Black Gap area, Texas. Right: Casa Grande in the Chisos Mountains, Texas

Burros, Boquillas, Mexico. Left: Boquillas Canyon, Big Bend National Park

Limestone wash in Black Gap, Texas

Ocotillo at Langtry, Texas

Fault in limestone cliff below Langtry

Tlalac, God of Rain, Ciudad Acuna, Mexico

Statue of St. Augustine, Patron of Laredo

Waterfall on Las Cuanas Creek, south of Eagle Pass, Texas

Thatch roof home at Jimenez, Mexico. Right: Old church tower in Camargo, Mexico

Spanish moss, Bentsen, Rio Grande Valley State Park. Left: a Chachalaca in the Santa Ana Refuge

Lower river rowboat

Hand drawn ferry, Los Banos, Texas

River bank, lower Rio Grande

Thatch roofed rancho buildings, near Campamento, Texas

Grapefruit, lower Rio Grande valley

La Lomita Museum of Fine Arts, formerly Oblate Fathers Novitiate

Shrimp nets at the Brownsville Shrimp Boat Basin. Right: Shrimp boat on the ways, Brownsville

Mouth of the Rio Grande and Washington Beach, Mexico. Left: Meandering Rio Grande near its mouth

Sand dunes, South Padre Island

Mexican fisherman at the Rio Grande mouth